Called Out

Nashunda Squier

Presentation by *BookLeaf Publishing*

Web: www.bookleafpub.com

E-mail: info@bookleafpub.com

ISBN: 9789357617062

First edition 2022

Lovingly dedicated to my husband, Mark,

for his unwavering belief in me,

and

the sacrifices he has made

so I can pursue my dreams.

ACKNOWLEDGEMENT

There are many people who have come into my life and contributed to my growth and successes. Every one of them deserves to be acknowledged, however, if I were to do that, the result would be longer than the remainder of this book.

Let me start off by saying thank you to my family and my friends who have been supportive and encouraging. Your belief in me has helped me continue on this journey. Also, I am beyond appreciative for each and every one of my brothers and sisters in Christ. You have each poured into me by following God's prompting and using your unique gifts, including those of you who helped to edit this book. You are each such a blessing.

That being said, there is one without whom this may not have come to fruition. So, Luke Ciraky, thank you for your faith, your obedience to God, and for being the hands and feet of Jesus. Your persistence introduced me to the only one who could provide my salvation, redeem me and restore me to wholeness. I am forever grateful.

Ultimately, all the glory goes to God. Thank you, Jesus, for my life, the purpose you created specifically for me, and for each person and thing you have provided along the way so that I may fulfill that purpose.

PREFACE

I have experienced darkness in my life. I have not only experienced it, but I've curled up and lived in it to the point where I couldn't tell where darkness ended and I began. The darkness that enveloped me was a product of the circumstances of my life and I am sure that there are circumstances in all of our lives that have the ability to pitch us into such an abyss. While yours may be the same, they also may be different, but nonetheless real and overwhelming for us to navigate.

I have learned, through my trials, that there is truth to the adages that state, "there is no light without darkness" or "you can't see the light without darkness". I could barely dream of light when I was in that place. However, the thing about light is, it travels. It knows no bounds and travels "light years" across all manner of obstacles to reach its destination, cast out darkness, and bring clarity of sight. That is powerful.

Is it any wonder, then, that God is light? Although I rejected Him for years, He persisted. He traveled through space and time and traversed the obstacle that I had become in my resistance of Him. He continued to lovingly pursue me; until He reached me, penetrated the darkness in which I resided, and brought light into my life.

Now, I have Good News for you. Regardless of the circumstances in your life, He can do the same for you. He has already chosen you. You are special to Him. I hope these poems lead to an opening in whatever darkness you are experiencing through which His light seeps in and calls you out into the warmth of His healing light.

"But you are a chosen people, a royal priesthood, a holy nation, God's special possession, that you may declare
the praises of him who called you out of darkness into his wonderful light."
1 Peter 2:9 (NIV)

Dark

Dead light
coming to life
for a split second
a spark, a flicker
of temporary movement
a slight buzz of breath
the last one though
no more light
dead once again

The Unforgiven To Remain Untold

Clues of the unforgiven
locked inside my heart
and covered with all the pain
always on the verge
of being revealed
yet always falling from the weight
of the continuous burden
that is thrown my way

My head aches
as thoughts float in its fog
lost and broken
craziness is what I retreat to
and all of my precious secrets
shall be buried
within the crevices of my depression
and they are dead
as similarly as my thoughts
my spirit, my mind
and so are to remain
forever untold

Absorbed

One can only dream
of an obscurity so vivid
that death embraces it;
yet as I stare into the eyes
of my mirrored reflection
I see that darkness
a bright black
as if there isn't any life left
for in them I see none…
only emptiness
an emptiness in which I am engrossed
in which I search for something…
for my self
to help me find my way back to life
but there is nothing
and I fall
through a black abyss
lost and gone

Runaway One

Afraid
of something and yet nothing
can't figure it out
don't even want to
trying to leave it behind
run to a fantasy
a life of perfection
can't escape reality
trapped in a meaningless reverie
unable to return
lost somewhere
still getting nowhere
at a standstill
in a private nightmare
running from what
not exactly clear
turn around and look back
wanting so much
to reach what's been pushed out of reach
but there is no turning back now…

The bridge is burned

A Good-bye Kiss

I stand
faceless
in a disorganized circle
amongst these so-called friends
waiting with ambivalence
as she makes her way toward me
seeing that everyone is entranced
by the beauty and tranquility
she brings with her
I watch as she kisses the one next to me
then I take her
grasping her tightly
and I kiss her so passionately
that I pull all air from her being
and into my own
sucking all life out of her
staying only to stare
at the ash she has left me to hold
I sigh
and happily yet sorrowfully
say good-bye
and as I exhale the last of her breath
my heart sinks

Love Me He Did

He saw me before him
and although he knew
that it could never be
I guess he had strange feelings
about him and me
or maybe they were only between
his multiple beings
of or regarding me
I do not know
maybe he wished he could love me
not just physically
but with everything that he knew

For he said of me
"But love her I shall"

"Love her with my thoughts
Love her with my heart and soul
Love her through love and peace and war
Love her through craziness
And love her through sanity
Love her
Love her
Love her with my words
Love her with my emotions and my dreams"

"Love her with my fists"

"Pounding, pounding
Pounding my love into her
Loving, pounding, hurting
Pain… that comes with love
She shall feel the pain of my love
And she shall bleed the blood of my love
Through all this, although I may hurt her
I love her… and love her I shall"

And in his way
this way
Love me he did

Ambivalence Of Emotions

In this atmosphere of overcast skies
indiscriminate tears fall
flowing into the secretions of daily life
blood, tears, sweat, and cum
a picturesque portrayal
of pain, sorrow, love, and lust
creating a scenario in which
all emotions become one
and are drowned

Trapped

In a room
the future becoming
as it has been many times before
will happen again
soon
too soon
all flashes before knowing eyes
past blending
with present
future
rushing towards
a fist of rage
promising
pain, blurred vision
it hurts
but laugh
shed no tears
just laugh
at the poor inhumane bastard
the asshole
that loves to see pain inflicted
another fist
all goes black

A dream of a place

alive
no fear
no pain
yet simply a dream
a virtual image
for in reality
pain may be all that is ever known

Hope Shatters

It floats
seemingly on the breeze
carried on the breath of promises
whispers of change
but how can hope linger
upon words unfulfilled?

When words are no longer as angels wings;
feathers that softly caress
love
but are rather
a constant reminder
of actions that never occur
like thorns, mini daggers
piercing
causing pain
as the heart and mind recall to memory
these words that have been uttered before
again, and again

They are worn and weak
they can no longer support hope
thus
it sinks
lower and lower

falling
shattered on the ground
crushed beneath the feet of inaction
waiting, longing
for something to be done
to mend and restore
hope

A Tiny Cry

Curled
beneath the safety of the covers
I stare
at blankness
as a solitary tear
pushes its way down my face
my silent plea
for help

Moments More To Go

On the threshold of a dream
days of future's past
of diamonds to rust
only moments more to go

Moments more to go
storm overhead
such is life
want to get away
depart from it all

Just remember
the coming of dawn

Dawn

Awake in darkness
to peer out at the sleeping world
in which gray hovers
and mist is suspended
enveloping the sounds
so that silence prevails
until a finger of the sun
pokes at the earth
urging it to wake

Seek Him

Stumbling through the darkness
frantically searching for what has become lost
how does one lose something like that
something as important as
identity
and yet its absent
disappeared and forgotten
like actors
who having played too many roles
no longer know who they are
I have acted my way through this life
but I have learned
that you will find what you are looking for
in the last place you look and I have nowhere
else
to turn
so in a last-ditch effort born of desperation
I turn to what I have rejected
for now it is time to do what they have said
"Seek Him and you will find yourself"

Let Go Let God

Hurt
passed down
accepted, grasped
taken to heart
and heart taken
hidden away
buried
in an illusion of protection
through which the Enemy continues
to run us through
with the inability to forgive
thus, the wounds remain
and the blood flows endless
Jesus, rescue me
I call to you
help me to forgive
release this stronghold of unforgiveness
bring my heart from darkness
I give it to you
set it free

From Water And Spirit

I am but a newborn
born new to faith
I look to you
and as a babe raises its arms to its mother
I raise my arms, to you, Father
beckoning
lift me up
hold me to you
teach me
for I know naught
take my hand
as a parent would a child
and lead me along the path

Embraced In Truth

In the breeze
I am young
pulled around
swayed and pushed
embraced in truth
kissed and caressed
by the wind
I am loved

On Our Own

In an infantile state of determination
we persist
pushing forward
struggling
in an attempt to achieve
on our own
we fight the obstacles,
the barriers that riddle the path
focusing on the "I"
wanting the accolades of success
a pat on the back
yearning so much for our worth to be seen
for recognition in what we accomplish
on our own
we stumble, we fall
we knock down others and clamor over them
we crawl
in this infantile state
rarely maturing to realize
that we are relational
not meant to be
on our own
that we could attain so much more
if only we would reach out, reach up
and accept assistance

What I Have Heard In Silence

With the world
away
I sit
surrounded by silence
yet there is much to be heard
from within myself
from this mind
that never truly quiets
What do I hear?
What is it I hear….
in this silence of self?
What does my heart whisper…
a cliché of love?
No, something more…

"I am here"
a call comes from the depths
"Listen"

This I hear,
Spirit
calling out in silence.

Though I Continue To Stumble

Though I continue to stumble
among the worldly obstacles
and I repeatedly fall short
there is one who knows and loves me

He's always there to pick me up
though I continue to stumble
extending both a helping hand
and a grace truly undeserved

He waits faithfully to catch me
meeting me wherever I am
though I continue to stumble
when my focus is not in Him

With eyes of a loving father
He looks at me with pride because
He sees in me a heart he loves
though I continue to stumble

Holy Metamorphosis

Children gather
on the banks of a wooded creek
with a hunger
insatiable
like caterpillars
crawling to and fro'
seeking to be filled
consuming many things
but none that satisfies
wounded, broken, and weak
staggering toward the water
weeping, thirsting
and again, like caterpillars
finally submitting to death
submerged in muddy water
dead and gone
but resurrected
emerging cleansed and transformed
dripping in newness
just as butterflies exiting their chrysalises
wholly beautiful
forever changed
never to be caterpillars again
and loosed to fly
in the world yet not of it

to be looked upon
and to share the glory
of the way, the truth, and the life.

Fibonacci Swirl

God
brings
swirling
not chaos
but order within
predestined movements of His will